STANDING FIRM

IN THE EVIL DAY

STANDING FIRM

IN THE EVIL DAY

Terry Bryant

Wyatt House Publishing

Mobile, Alabama

Wyatt House books may be ordered through booksellers or by contacting:

WYATT HOUSE PUBLISHING
399 Lakeview Dr. W.
Mobile, Alabama 36695
www.wyattpublishing.com
editor@wyattpublishing.com

Because of the dynamic nature of the Internet, any web address or links contained in this book may have changed since publication and may no longer be valid.

Cover design by: Mark Wyatt
Interior design by: Mark Wyatt

ISBN 13:978-1-954798-06-9

Printed in the United States of America

DEDICATION

This book is dedicated to my wife, Sherry, who has stood by me for 47 years. She is a strong woman of faith and commitment. I could not have accomplished the things I have in my ministry without her love and support.

Special thanks also goes to Mark Waynick for his help in the preparation of this book.

FOREWORD

Wisdom is the principal thing;
Therefore get wisdom.
And in all your getting, get understanding.

(Proverbs 4:7, NKJV)

I first met Brother Terry in the mid-1990s at a revival in Texas. Terry got saved as a senior in high school. He was called to preach soon after. For the last 50 years or so he has led youth groups, college groups, pastored churches, been an evangelist, bible study teacher and has been, and is, a mentor to men. Now the Lord has put it in his heart to be an author. This book is his first, of what I hope will be many.

I was a young believer and loved the Lord when I first met Terry. Being young in the Lord, I had a lot of sin issues. To me, it seemed I had more issues than my contemporaries. I needed a lot of help. I knew I needed help and so did those around me. Brother Terry preached that revival in Texas and it seemed to me that he had answers for what was going on in my heart. I needed what this man knew about God and His word! I began to pray and ask the Lord to let me get close to Terry so I could hear more of what this man had learned. God answered that prayer. I have been able to hear him preach many times and been blessed to listen to many of his sermons on tape. But more than that, God saw fit to bless me by letting me sit at Terry's feet for almost 30 years. Many of my victories in life are due to Terry teaching me about God. Through my many failures, God and Brother Terry have been faithful.

The impact on my life is indescribable. My growth was very slow at times and incredibly fast at others. Some battles were easy and others were hard. Terry was patient with me. I had bible knowledge but not biblical understanding. What do I mean by that? Well, I knew some verses, some passages but I did not understand them properly. And because my understanding was wrong, I was not able to walk in the power of the Holy Spirit the way God desired and provided for. There are so many things Terry taught me. Terry taught me the value of wisdom, about warfare, God's great mercy, and to walk in the fear of God.

Terry taught me that true wisdom is seeing things from God's perspective. When I saw things from God's viewpoint, I began to understand His ways.I found purpose and power in God's wisdom. In this book on Ephesians written by Brother Terry, you will find it full of God's perspective about who you are in Christ, how to walk worthy of your calling in Christ, and how to have power to stand in Christ in the evil day. Terry would say "sit, walk, stand" and "our position in Christ, our practice in Christ, and our protection in Christ". He would also add "The bible is not just for our head knowledge, or understanding. The bible is something we should experience inwardly, in our hearts, so that we can walk it out in our life."

All of us have experienced evil days. Jesus experienced many of them. But he was secure in the knowledge of who He was to the Father. He walked with God and did not sin. In the great evil days in the desert, Gethsemane, and on the cross Jesus stood firm. Because Jesus stood in the evil days, you can too by the grace of God and the power of the Holy Spirit. God has provided for us, through Christ, so that we can stand not only in the present evil day, but in our personal trials and yes, even in the end times.

May this book be a great blessing to you. May the Lord God give us all a view of things as He sees them. May we understand how He sees us and may we walk in the full knowledge of His victory and His love. And may we all stand firm in the evil day.

Mark Waynick

In Their Words...

I have known Terry Bryant for fifty years. It has been my privilege to watch him live out God's call to ministry in his life. We were both called to ministry under Dr. Fred Wolfe, long time pastor of Cottage Hill Baptist Church in Mobile, Alabama. He and I have shared the good times and the challenges of ministry. He has not only been a dear friend but a mentor and counselor through the years we have known each other. Brother Terry is a gifted communicator and preacher. I know God will use this book to encourage you in your walk with the Lord.

Rev. John Turner
Pastor, Ingalls Avenue Baptist Church
Pascagoula, Mississippi

Terry Bryant has been one of my favorite preachers for many years. He illuminates scripture with scripture, the result of which is a deeper understanding of God and His Word. I have never stumped him a single time with a Bible question. And I love that his life reflects what he preaches. This book will be by my most comfortable chair and a great companion.

Brad Sutton,
Pastor, Point Church
Dallas, Texas

I have followed Terry Bryant's ministry for over 30 years and can testify that God has gifted my friend with great insight into God's word. As followers of Christ, knowing the days we live in we need to hear the Lord. Terry has a unique gift for communicating God's message to God's children to bring clarity, encouragement, and hope to those who trust in God.

Alan Wright
Former Assoc. Pastor, South Lakeland Baptist Church
Lakeland, Florida

Our lives were forever changed through the leadership and teaching of Brother Terry. We received revelation through Brother Terry's teaching of the word. We learned to love the Lord and hear the Holy Spirit. I am so very grateful!

Rhonda Medley
Dental Hygienist
Fayetteville, Tennessee

Through the years that I've known him, Brother Terry has always been there when I needed prayer or Godly advice. He encouraged me with God's word. He is more than generous with his time and is rich in God's Word. He shares it freely whenever someone needs encouraging. I am so blessed to be on his daily devotional list and cannot wait to be reading his book.

Donna Dillard
Real Estate Agent
Blairsville, Georgia

CHAPTER 1
THE SIGNS OF THE TIMES

The Last Days

There is little disagreement that we're living in the last days. The signs of the times are everywhere and in abundance. This book is not focused on prophecy of the end times but rather how to stand firm in Christ in the last days.

People have many ideas on preparing for the last days. Some build bunkers, store lots of food and water, buy guns and ammo, start living off the grid, etc. I am not saying any of that is wrong. It just doesn't prepare the believer for the last days. We can have all the natural provisions and yet not be prepared. What we need more than anything is to be prepared spiritually. And one way to be prepared is to be spiritually aware of what is working in the world today. The Apostle John said:

1 John 4: 1, 3 *"Beloved, do not believe every spirit, but test the spirits to see whether they are from God...and every spirit that does not confess Jesus is not from God; this is the spirit of the antichrist, of which you have heard that is coming, and now it is already in the world."*

The spirit of the antichrist is most definitely moving in our day and it will test the believer. The opposition to the children of God is becoming unprecedented. We now see this opposition turning more violent. It will get to the point where we will see more martyrs. Matthew 24:8 says, this time will be called "the beginning of sorrows." The question each believer must ask themselves is "Are we prepared?"

We will be studying through the book of Ephesians to see what the Apostle Paul says about standing firm in the evil day. It is my prayer that each person that reads this book, takes what Paul teaches to heart. The body of Christ needs to be prepared for the last days.

Signs of the Times

I have decided to mention a few key signs of the last days. This will illustrate the fact that we are not looking for the last days but realizing they are upon us now.

Daniel 12:4 *"But as for you, Daniel, conceal these words and seal up the book until the end of time..."*

The book of Daniel contains prophecies concerning the end of time. In the above verse, God is informing the prophet Daniel that these prophecies are concealed or hidden until the last days. There will be a generation living in the last days that will see and understand the fulfillment of these prophecies. Then God lists two signs of the end of time.

1. The Sign of Increased Travel

Daniel 12:4 *"...seal up the book until the end of time; many will go back and forth..."*

There will be an explosion of travel in the end of time. That's our generation. It used to take many months to travel from the east coast to the west coast by horse and buggy. Now you can travel across the country in a few hours on a plane. It is even possible to fly across the world in a matter of hours. We've sent men to the moon and back and Voyager 1 is all the way out in interstellar space. Travel has exploded in our generation.

2. The Sign of Increase in knowledge

Daniel 12:4 *"...many will go back and forth, and knowledge will increase."*

Here again, man's knowledge has exploded. Someone said man's knowledge up until the early 19th century, if measured, would be 3 inches. From the 19th century until now it would measure the height of the Washington Monument. Even our cell phones can be upgraded about once a year if we desire to keep up with the technology that is being developed. Knowledge on every subject is exploding.

3. The Sign of Israel

The prophet Isaiah, wrote that something was going to happen that had never happened before. A nation would be established in a day, without war.

Isaiah 66:7-8 *"Before she travailed, she brought forth; Before her pain came, she gave birth to a boy. Who has heard such a thing? Who has seen such things? Can a land be born in one day? Can a nation be brought forth all at once?*

As soon as Zion travailed, she also brought forth her sons."

Here was a mystery hidden through the years. What was the prophet talking about? It is not a mystery anymore. On May 14th, 1948 the establishment of the State of Israel was declared and the U.S. President, Harry S. Truman, recognized the new nation on the same day. Because of the suffering the Jewish people endured, the world established the state of Israel in a day. The prophecy was fulfilled in our generation. This is a big, big sign.

4. *The Sign of Violence*

Jesus speaking to His disciples, answering their question about the end of time, stated it will be like in the days of Noah.

Matthew 24:37, *"For the coming of the Son of Man will be just like the days of Noah."*

Those days were marked by violence.

Genesis 6:11, *"...and the earth was filled with violence."*

Genesis 6:13 *Then God said to Noah, "The end of all flesh has come before Me; for the earth is filled with violence because of them; and behold, I am about to destroy them with the earth."*

Kings and people with absolute authority have always oppressed their people. Now we are seeing globally a generation where the common man is violent. The Bible says:

Genesis 6:5-6 *Then the Lord saw that the wickedness of man was great on the earth, and that every intent of the thoughts of his heart was only evil continually. The Lord was sorry that He had made man on the earth, and He was grieved in His heart.*

Again, Jesus stated it would be just like it was in the days of Noah in that last generation before He comes. It is not my desire to go into graphic details of the violence taking place today. All one needs to do is to listen to what's being reported daily. And that's not all the violence taking place. There are tens of thousands of horrific acts of violence that no one is reporting. God sees them all and it breaks his heart.

As the world rejects the Gospel of Jesus' love and forgiveness, their hearts are getting harder and growing cold.

5. The Sign of Sexual Perversion.

Luke 17:28-30 *"It was the same as happened in the days of Lot... but on that day that Lot went out of Sodom it rained fire and brimstone from heaven and destroyed them all. 30 It will be just the same on the day that the Son of Man is revealed."*

Lot's days were days of sexual perversions. Genesis 19 records the story of the two angels who were sent to check out the sinful cries of Sodom and Gomorrah. The men of the city were wicked and perverted. And were trying to storm the door of Lot's house to get the two men who were angels. Lot offered his virgin daughters to the men. But they had no interest in the daughters because their passion burned for men. So perverted were those cities that God destroyed them both with fire and brimstone. It will be like the days of Lot before the coming of the Son of Man. This wickedness is not restricted to a couple of cities but has spread worldwide in our generation.

These are but a few of the signs of the end of time. We need to be able to stand firm in the evil day. Stand strong in Christ and his righteousness and strength.

Luke 21:28 *"But when these things begin to take place, straighten up and lift up your heads, because your redemption is drawing near."*

When Jesus came the first time, He came in mercy and grace. He came to forgive and to pardon. And the world abused Him. They lied about Him. They framed Him. They mocked Him. And they ultimately crucified Him. The second coming of Jesus will not be in mercy. He is coming for justice and judgment. He is coming to judge the entire Godless world for their Godless deeds. He came as a servant the first time. Next time, He is coming as a judge. He came as a lamb and is coming as a lion. The first time He came we slayed Him. The next time He comes, He will slay the wicked. He will show no mercy and give no grace. Only those who have been redeemed by the blood of the Lamb will be spared the wrath of God.

Chapter 2
UNDERSTANDING OUR POSITION IN CHRIST

Ephesians can be divided into 3 sections; *sit, walk and stand,* or *our position in Christ, our practice in Christ* and *our protection in Christ.*

Notice how many times the little phrase "in Christ" is used in Ephesians 1:

v.3 "in Christ",
v.7 " in Him",
v.13 "in Him, in Him".

This is telling us that our position is in Christ. These verses state that we are seated with Him in heavenly places.

SECTION 1: WE ARE BLESSED!

Ephesians 1:3 *Blessed be the God and Father of our Lord Jesus Christ, who has blessed us with every spiritual blessing in the heavenly places in Christ...*

This verse says, we have everything we will ever need in Christ, who lives in us and through us. Let me say it again, we have everything we will ever need in Christ, who lives in us and through us.

In other words, the way God sees and responds to Christ is the same way God sees and responds to us. We are blessed! We have His righteousness, His wisdom and His power. Everything we need spiritually we have because of our position in Christ. Remember the Bible says:

Colossians 3:3 *For you have died and your life is hidden with Christ in God.*

SECTION 2: WE ARE CHOSEN!

In Ephesians 1:4 we see a concept that is very difficult to fully understand, that of being chosen by God.

Ephesians 1:4: *… just as He chose us in Him before the foundation of the world…*

This means before God created this world, before God ever created mankind, God chose the believer to be in Christ. Now, that very concept is deep and beyond our comprehension. We may ask how? How did God know I would choose to follow Christ? Because He is all knowing, ever present and all powerful. God is not limited to time and space as we are. We are so limited in our understanding. God is forever reminding us that we understand nothing.

Job 38:4 *"Where were you when I laid the foundation of the earth? Tell Me, if you have understanding."*

In Job chapter 38, God asked Job a series of questions. Who controls the seas? Who commands the morning dawn? Can you understand the vastness of this universe? And the answer is no. Man has no idea how much a mountain weighs or the number of stars in the universe and their names; all of which God knows. The Christian life is not one of figuring out God, then believing. It is trusting Him then He gives us understanding and the ability to know Him.

What an absolute blessing to know that God "...chose us in Christ before the foundation of the world." And not only chose us but that we would stand holy and blameless before Him

Ephesians 1:4 ... *just as He chose us in Him...that we would be holy and blameless before Him.*

In other words, God not only chose us but He fixed us.

SECTION 3: WE ARE PREDESTINED

Ephesians 1: 5 *He predestined us to adoption as sons through Jesus Christ to Himself, according to the kind intention of His will...*

Notice four powerful words in verse 5: "predestined", "adoption" and "kind intention." God has always had a plan for His beloved; those He knew would one day come to the end of themselves and surrender to the

Lordship of Christ. They would see their fallen state before God and repent, putting their faith in Christ. Those He chose, He predestined to be something special.

What is that something special? Notice the second word, **adoption**. He chose us to be sons of the Most High God. God actually becomes our Father in Heaven. Remember, when the disciples asked Jesus, "Lord, teach us to pray"? He answered them this way:

Matthew 6:9: *Pray, then, in this way:*
'Our Father who is in heaven,
Hallowed be Your name...'

Jesus was teaching them that God is their Father. How is this possible? They were adopted as sons through being born again spiritually, a new birth.

And lastly, notice the statement "according to the **kind intention** of His will." God does all of this out of love and the kind intentions of His heart. Understand, God does not have to do any of this. He could leave all of us in a fallen state to be judged without mercy. But according to His will, He chose not to do so. We can understand now why Paul breaks out in praise!

Ephesians 1:6 *To the praise of the glory of His grace, wherein He hath made us accepted in the Beloved.* (KJV)

He freely gave this wonderful privilege to us, the adoption as sons. Don't take God's kindness for granted. Live like a child of the Most High God. All of this happens when we are born again. Jesus said "unless a man is born again, he cannot enter the kingdom of God"

John 3:7 *"Do not be amazed that I said to you, 'You must be born again.'"*

The new birth is possible because God deals with our sin problem.

SECTION 4: WE ARE REDEEMED

Ephesians 1:7-8 *In Him we have redemption through His blood, the forgiveness of our trespasses, according to the riches of His grace which He lavished on us...*

<u>Man's Condition Before Redemption:</u>

(1) Man is dead spiritually.

Ephesians 2:1 *And you were dead in your trespasses and sins...*

Man died the day Adam sinned against God in the garden. God stated:

Gen 2:17b *"...for in the day that you eat from it you will surely die."*

Adam and Eve ate from that tree. And they died that day spiritually and eventually they died physically. From that day on, mankind was spiritually dead; dead to God, dead to His Spirit and dead to understanding His will. That is every man's condition today without Christ.

(2) Man acts like the world.

Ephesians 2:2a *in which you formerly walked according to the course of this world...*

Paul is saying, when a person is dead spiritually, they walk like the world, talk like the world and love the things the world loves (usually themselves).

(3) Man is under Satan's control.

Paul says the unredeemed are under the control of the devil.

Ephesians 2:2b *according to the prince of the power of the air, of the spirit that is now working in the sons of disobedience.*

In reality every unbeliever is controlled by Satan. They are in bondage to the kingdom of darkness. And they must be set free from Satan's grip. Only Jesus Christ has the power to accomplish this.

(4) Man is driven by the lust of the flesh.

Notice Paul says those that are spiritually dead, live for the lust of the flesh.

Ephesians 2:3 *Among them we too all formerly lived in the lusts of our flesh, indulging the desires of the flesh and of the mind, and were by nature children of wrath...*

When someone is spiritually dead, they live for the physical. They indulge in the lust of the flesh. That's because they are dead inside. They are trying to fill that void, that sense of emptiness. However, it doesn't work. Christ is the only answer.

Paul continues to give us insight into how God fixed mankind's problem through redemption. Paul gives us four insights into God's plan; The mystery of redemption, the plan of redemption, the motive of redemption and the results of redemption.

The Mystery of Redemption: The Cross

God has a mystery which He made known through the written word, and the preaching of the gospel.

Ephesians 1:9a *He made known to us the mystery of His will...*

But what was the mystery?

The mystery is the redemption of man through the cross, the new birth, and the adoption as sons. Unless God opens the eyes of our understanding, we would never see His plan for us. This is why it's so important to preach and teach the Word of God.

Romans 10:14 *"How then will they call on Him in whom they have not believed? How will they believe in Him whom they have not heard? And how will they hear without a preacher?"*

The gospel that we preach is based upon Christ and His blood. The whole reason for His death on the cross was for the sins of the world.

John 3:17 *For God did not send the Son into the world to judge the world, but that the world might be saved through Him.*

Let's make it personal. He died for your sins and mine. Forgiveness is a beautiful word when you stand guilty before God Almighty, the Righteous Judge. All of our transgressions and sins are cleansed by His blood when we put our faith in Him.

Why would Jesus die for us?

Ephesians 1:7 *...according to the riches of His grace.*

Again, God loves us and is rich in mercy and grace. The Bible says "his lovingkindness and tender mercies are new and fresh every morning".

Lamentations 3:22-23:
The Lord's lovingkindnesses indeed never cease,
For His compassions never fail.
23 They are new every morning;
Great is Your faithfulness.

He also states that His abundant grace is lavished upon us. The word picture is as if God is pouring out His blessings so that our cup is full and overflowing. Hallelujah!!! Let us enjoy every day His abundant grace.

The Plan of Redemption: Establish His Kingdom

God's plan is to establish His kingdom on the earth.

Ephesians 1: 10 ...*with a view to an administration suitable to the fullness of the times, that is, the summing up of all things in Christ, things in the heavens and things on the earth...*

Again, this is a part of His mystery. God's plan is to establish His kingdom on earth as it is in heaven. Remember, Jesus taught His disciples to pray this prayer:

Matthew 6:10 *Your kingdom come,*
Your will be done,
On earth as it is in heaven.

God is going to establish His physical kingdom when He returns. But until then He is establishing His spiritual kingdom in the hearts and minds of believers who trust in Him.

The Motive of Redemption: Love

God always has a motive for the things He does. Here God again establishes His motivation is love.

Ephesians 1:9b *...according to His kind intention which He purposed in Him*

Everything God is doing He's doing out of love and compassion. God is working His master plan in us through Christ. He is establishing His rule in our lives. There is a battle that takes place each day. The battle is between God and the devil, the flesh and spirit, the physical and the spiritual. Part of God's plan to establish His kingdom in us is destroying our self-rule. This may take us down many different paths and some are very difficult because denying self is not easy. But the mature child of

God sees and understands the ways of God. He will ultimately yield to the will of God because he understands God is doing all of this out of love and His way is best.

Results of Redemption: Obtained an Inheritance

Ephesians 1:10b-11 *In Him also we have obtained an inheritance, having been predestined according to His purpose who works all things after the counsel of His will*

Remember we have been predestined to be sons of the Most High God. As sons we have an inheritance. The concept of inheritance is very important in the Bible, not only in transferring wealth and substance to the next generation but more importantly, it is the transferring of spiritual wealth and gifts to God's children. And all of this is possible because we are "in Him".

SECTION 5: WE ARE SEALED

Ephesians 1:13 *In Him, ... having also believed, you were sealed in Him with the Holy Spirit of promise...*

The sanctifying and comforting work of the Holy Spirit sealed the believer as an heir of heaven. This is a part of our inheritance. The greatest evidence that you are a true child of God is the Holy Spirit in your life. The fullness of God dwells in us in the person of the Holy Spirit.

Ephesians 1:14a *who is given as a pledge of our inheritance...*

Every believer who has the Holy Spirit living in them has the mark of God in them. The Holy Spirit will conform us to the image of the Lord Jesus. We now have His nature and His heart. Again, Paul breaks into praise and adoration.

Ephesians 1:14c *...to the praise of His glory.*

Let us also praise Him for His wonderful plan of salvation. And let's not forget the importance of understanding who we are in Christ.

Spiritual Warfare Insight: Understanding your position on the battlefield is of utmost importance. We have a positional advantage. We are in Christ!

CHAPTER 3
UNDERSTANDING OUR PRACTICE IN CHRIST

This part of Ephesians deals with our walk in Christ. Notice in chapter 4 of Ephesians how Paul transitions into a new theme. Ephesians 4:1 starts with the word, "Therefore". It is as though Paul is saying "Now that we have established the fact that your position is in Christ. Act like it. Walk like it. Live like it. Walk in a manner worthy of sonship."

Ephesians 4:1 *Therefore I, the prisoner of the Lord, implore you to walk in a manner worthy of the calling with which you have been called...*

Paul is imploring them to act like sons of the Most High God. We cannot have a faith that just believes. The Bible calls that dead faith. We must have a faith that acts. True faith in Christ will affect our walk. It will affect the way we think, the way we talk and the way we behave. You may not be perfect but you will be changed. And you will walk differently.

Ephesians 5:17 *So then do not be foolish, but understand what the will of the Lord is.*

So many people wonder what God's will is for their lives. God answers in Ephesians. Being in Christ will affect one's walk (behavior) in several ways. You will see this in five basic areas:

1. In Relation to the Old Man
2. In Relation to Righteousness
3. In Relation to the Holy Spirit
4. In Relation to Spiritual Authority in the Family
5. In Relation to Spiritual Authority Outside the Family

God has made His will very clear in Ephesians.

In Relation to the Old Man

One of the wonderful things that happens, when an individual is born again, is the old man is put to death. He has no more dominion over you. Can the old fleshly habits still affect us? Yes. If you don't reckon self as crucified with Christ each day, the old fleshly temptations can cause you to stumble. Remember that Jesus said:

Luke 9:23 *And He was saying to them all, "If anyone wants to come after Me, he must deny himself, take up his cross daily, and follow Me."*

Jesus is stating that He is going to be Lord of your life, or you are going to be the lord of your life. In order to follow Him, you must deny yourself daily. Jesus and Paul are saying the same thing and both are emphasizing that we have to deal with our self-life and give up our self-rule.

It's a battle we face every day. Whereas before there was no battle and the old man had total dominion over us. Paul is encouraging the young believers to put off the old man and to put on the new man and walk in righteousness.

Ephesians 4:22,24 *... that, in reference to your former manner of life, you lay aside the old self... and put on the new self, which in the likeness of God has been created in righteousness and holiness of the truth.*

Now Paul goes into detail describing what the old self looks like.

(1) Speech

(a) Falsehoods and lies

Ephesians 4:25a *Therefore, laying aside falsehood, speak truth each one of you with his neighbor...*

Unfortunately, that is not how this world operates. They will lie about everything. As a matter of fact, it's hard to find the truth today. Politicians, Media, News outlets, Corporations, Pharmaceutical companies, etc. all are very deceitful. God is saying if you're born again from above stop lying to people. Speak the truth.

(b) Unwholesome Words

Ephesians 4:29a *Let no unwholesome word proceed from your mouth...*

The phrase "unwholesome words" means speech that tears down and does not build up. Don't let that kind of speech come out of your mouth. So, what kind of words does God want us to use? God wants us to speak edifying words which do build up moral character.

Ephesians 4:29b *...but only such a word as is good for edification...*

We are to speak words that lift up, build up and strengthen one's character and to encourage others to succeed.

James 3:10 ... *from the same mouth come both blessing and cursing. My brethren, these things should not be this way.*

Proverbs 18:21a *Death and life are in the power of the tongue*

God is clearly telling us that we have power with the spoken word. We can speak life or we can speak death. We can speak blessings or we can speak curses. Make sure your speech is edifying and speaking life.

Ephesians 4:29c *...according to the need of the moment, so that it will give grace to those that hear."*

God is saying let your speaking be seasoned with grace. As a cook adds seasoning to the food for flavor, so add grace to your speech for edification.

Ephesians 5:4 *and there must be no filthiness and silly talk, or coarse jesting, which are not fitting, but rather giving thanks.*

We are to be imitators of God as beloved children. These works of the old man are not God's will for the believer. God says that what is in the heart will come out of your mouth.

Luke 6:45b *...for his mouth speaks from that which fills his heart*

So, if filthy talk and coarse jesting is coming out of your mouth, guess what? The old self is in control of your life and the Holy Spirit is grieved. Our speech needs to be full of gratitude for the many blessings God has poured upon us.

(2) Be not angry in the flesh

Ephesians 4:26 *Be angry, and yet do not sin; do not let the sun go down on Your anger*

You cannot observe the evil that happens every day and not be angry. But don't get in the flesh and respond wrongly. You can be upset at the injustice and evil without sinning. If you let anger control you, you will give the devil an open door and opportunity to attack your life.

Ephesians 4:27 *Neither give place to the devil.* (KJV)

(3) Don't steal

Ephesians 4:28a *He who steals must steal no longer...*

Paul says, work with your hands, in order to have enough so you can share with others. We labor in order to help, not only ourselves, but others. Stop stealing! These activities describe the old man's lifestyle.

(4) Bitterness

Ephesians 4:31 *Let all bitterness and wrath and anger and clamor and slander be put away from you along with all malice.*

Bitterness is when someone gets hurt or offended and will not let it go. But if we choose to hold on to the offense it will become a deep root of bitterness. This only hurts the embittered person. It can only lead to outbursts of fleshly anger which can be physical violence or verbal violence. Slander is designed to destroy someone's character with words. Notice, right in the middle of all this fleshly action that God says something powerful: Give no place to the devil.

(5) Immorality

Ephesians 5:3 *"But immorality or any impurity or greed must not even be named among you, as is proper among saints;*

Ephesians 5:5 *"For this you know with certainty, that no immoral or impure person or covetous man, who is an idolater, has an inheritance in the kingdom of Christ and God."*

We must not only put away bitterness but also immorality of any kind. Immoral conduct is not to be named among you as saints of the Most-High God. God's will is very clear about immorality.

Paul is driving this fact home, that you cannot practice sin and still enter the kingdom of heaven. I didn't say you can't sin. You will not practice sin. Paul says that the man who holds on to his sin is an idolater. He loves his sin more than Christ.

Ephesians 5:6-7 *Let no one deceive you with empty words, for because of these things the wrath of God comes upon the sons of disobedience. 7 Therefore do not be partakers with them;*

It is as though God is firing a warning shot across the bow. Do not be deceived. If you think like the ungodly and walk like the ungodly, your place will be with the ungodly. Do not travel down that road, the road of destruction. Again, put off the old man and put on the new every day and be thankful.

(6) Grieve not the Spirit

Eph 4:30 *Do not grieve the Holy Spirit of God, by whom you were sealed for the day of redemption.*

God is saying that these actions of the flesh grieve the Spirit of the Living God. We are commanded not to grieve the Holy Spirit. He is our only hope for walking in a manner worthy of our calling. It is the power of the Holy Spirit that enables us to walk as children of the Most-High God.

In Relation to Righteousness

Just as God said to put off the old man, He also says we must put on the new man.

In the 5th chapter of Ephesians, the word "walk" is used three times:

v.2 "...and walk in love..."
v.8 "...walk as children of the light..."
v.15 "...walk not as unwise men but as wise."

1) Walk in Love

Ephesians 5:1-2 *Therefore be imitators of God, as beloved children; and walk in love, just as Christ also loved you and gave Himself up for us, an offering and a sacrifice to God a fragrant aroma.*

God's will for believers, is to put on the new man which is a walk of love. Jesus, our example, walked in love. We are commanded to imitate Him.

Ephesians 4:32 *Be kind to one another, tender-hearted, forgiving each other, just as God in Christ also has forgiven you.*

It is impossible to show the love of God to people you are angry with. God's answer is forgiveness just like He forgave us, we are to forgive one another. Then you are free to demonstrate kindness, tenderness and the love of Christ. Another way to say this is the same way God showed us mercy, we are to show mercy to others.

2) Walk in Light

Paul is discussing the believers walk in Christ. He tells the believers to walk as children of light. Notice how Paul discusses this subject.

Ephesians 5:8a *For you were formerly darkness, but now you are light in the Lord...*

Paul tells us our former lifestyle was lived in spiritual darkness and ignorance. We had no understanding of God's will or His ways. And we lived a life of sin and rebellion. But now the Lord has raised us from the dead, and from spiritual darkness, to live as children of light. We are to walk in the light of the Lord. Now we can understand and know what the will of God is, and walk in a way that is pleasing to Him. Again, listen to Paul's exhortation.

Ephesians 5:11 *Do not participate in the unfruitful deeds of darkness, but instead even expose them.*
Ephesians 5:13a *But all things become visible when they are exposed by the light...*

What is Paul saying? The Bible says that the Word of God is light.

Palms 119:105 *Thy word is a lamp unto my feet, and a light to my path.* (KJV)

The word of God is our light. The life of Christ is our light. Let the word of God expose the deeds of darkness and put them away from you as a child of God. That's the will of God concerning you.

3) Walk in Wisdom

Ephesians 5:15 *Therefore be careful how you walk, not as unwise men but as wise...*

When we put on the new man, we will walk differently. Not in former darkness, but as children of love, light and wisdom. God's word brings light. Light brings understanding. Understanding brings wisdom. Walk as wise men in the light.

Why is God spending so much time dealing with the deeds of the flesh? *Because all of these deeds will cause you to fall in the battle against the powers of darkness. You cannot walk in the flesh and have victory over the devil.*

IN RELATION TO THE HOLY SPIRIT

Ephesians 5:17 is the key verse to understanding our walk in Christ.

Ephesians 5:17 *So then do not be foolish, but understand what the will of the Lord is.*

The Apostle Paul is saying do not let the old desires control you. Rather, let the new man control you. What is he talking about?

Ephesians 5:18 *And do not get drunk with wine, for that is dissipation but be filled with the Spirit.*
("Dissipation" means *excess* or *reckless*)

In this passage there are two verbs, "do not get drunk" with wine and "be filled" with the Spirit. Everything else in this passage describes what happens to a person who is filled with the Spirit. We are to empty ourselves of self and be filled with the Spirit of God. Putting on the new self or new man means to be controlled by the Holy Spirit. And when a person is filled with the Spirit they are speaking, singing, and making music. They're always giving thanks to God out of a grateful heart. There is a joy that controls their lives and is expressed by singing, and making melody. Why would someone react like that? Remember your old life of being controlled by sin, darkness and the devil is over. A new life of righteousness and freedom is ours when God's Holy Spirit dwells in us. It's awesome to experience. You were dead. Now you're alive in Christ. That is something to sing and shout about!

Ephesians 5:20 ... *always giving thanks for all things in the name of our Lord Jesus Christ to God, even the Father.*

The Holy Spirit's presence in the believer's life, is our power to walk like Christ. He is our power to imitate God. Because it is actually God's life in us, living His life through us, once we are out of the way. Remember and understand what the will of the Lord is! Do not be controlled by fleshly desires but be filled with the Holy Spirit.

IN RELATION TO SPIRITUAL AUTHORITY IN THE FAMILY

We have seen God's will for our lives in relation to the old man, in relation to righteousness and in relation to the Holy Spirit. Now Paul covers our family life.

Paul starts with submission to authority in the family. Why? That's where most problems originate from. Wives' refusal to be subject to their husbands, children's refusal to obey their parents, and husbands who refuse to submit to God and love their wives.

I have been a pastoral counselor for 47 years. I understand why Paul, in dealing with the family, covered spiritual authority. That's the main conflict in a family. God is not dumb. He started with authority because that is the major issue.

Ephesians 5:22-23 *Wives, be subject to your own husbands, as to the Lord. For the husband is the head of the wife, as Christ also is the head of the church, He Himself being the Savior of the body.*

Here, God is giving us the chain of command in the family. God made Adam first. Then, God made Eve for Adam, to be a helpmate for him. And then came children who are subject to their parents.

Ephesians 6:1 *Children, obey your parents in the Lord, for this is right.*

Family authority is not a very popular subject matter in the modern-day church. But it is a major topic with God. God hates rebellion in His children in any form. Wives rebelling against husbands, children rebelling against parents and husbands rebelling against their spiritual authority, God.

Proverbs 17:11 *A rebellious man seeks only evil, So a cruel messenger will be sent against him.*

Every time Israel rebelled against God's word, God raised up the enemy to chasten his children. He hates rebellion in His children. Listen, don't let rebellion get in your heart in any form, or a cruel messenger will be sent to you.

When the family functions as God intended for it to function, the family is healthy. Now let's observe the roles of the family.

1. WIVES

Ephesians 5:24 *But as the church is subject to Christ, so also the wives ought to be to their husbands in everything.*

The duty of the wives is submission to their husbands as to the Lord. This means honoring and obeying their husbands as they would Christ.

2. HUSBANDS

Ephesians 5:28a *So husbands ought also to love their own wives as their own bodies.*

Husbands are to love their wives as their own body as Christ loved His own body, the church. The duty of the husband is to love his wife with a Christlike love. Seeing her as a part of himself. Treating her in the same manner as he would his own body. For example, if his body was sick, he would care for it and nourish it.

3. CHILDREN

Ephesians 6:1-3 *Children, obey your parents in the Lord, for this is right. Honor your father and mother... so that it may be well with you, and that you may live long on the earth.*

Children are to honor and obey their parents, so it may be well with them and they may live long on this earth.

I am not going into detail into the roles and functions of the family. I am only covering the chain of command or the structure of spiritual authority. Why? Because rebellion opens the door for the enemy to cause havoc in our lives. Remember Proverbs 17:11?

Proverbs 17:11 *A rebellious man seeks only evil,*
So a cruel messenger will be sent against him.

IN RELATION TO SPIRITUAL AUTHORITY OUTSIDE THE FAMILY

In Ephesians 6, Paul continues to address spiritual authority. He begins to explain the relationship between masters and slaves. In our day it's the relationship between employer and employees.

Ephesians 6:5 *Slaves, be obedient to those who are your masters according to the flesh, with fear and trembling, in the sincerity of your heart, as to Christ;*

The phrase "according to the flesh", means those who have authority over you in the natural like the police, government, employers, etc. Listen to the wording, "...with fear and trembling, in the sincerity of your heart..." Why so serious? Because a rebellious heart will be dealt with severely. Rebellion opens the door to demonic attacks.

Ephesians 4:27 *Neither give place to the devil.* (KJV)

Paul is saying this is a huge matter. It is an important truth we must understand and obey. The attitude of the servant is to be one of sincerity. It cannot be, what Paul calls, eye service.

Ephesians 6:6 ... *not by way of eyeservice, as men-pleasers, but as slaves of Christ, doing the will of God from the heart.*

It is God's will we learn to submit to spiritual authority from the heart. This provides evidence of a yielded heart. Remember the example of David and king Saul in the cave. David was the new anointed, upcoming king of Israel. But God had not established him yet. Saul was still king of Israel. The King, out of jealously, pursued David trying to kill him. The bible says that both Saul and David were in a cave one night. When Saul was asleep, David came upon Saul and could have killed him. Instead, David cut his garment. This let Saul know that David could have taken his life. But the moment David cut Saul's sash, the Spirit of God convicted David.Notice what happened to David:

1 Samuel 24:5 *And it came to pass afterward, that David's heart smote him, because he had cut off Saul's skirt.* (KJV)

Why did David's heart smite him? Because of what God said in Chronicles.

1 Chronicles 16:22 ... *Saying, "Touch not mine anointed, and do my prophets no harm."* (KJV)

Understand that Saul's positional anoniting as King had nothing to do with his character. They are two different anointings. There's an anointing of the Holy Spirit with power. Then there is an anointing with position of authority. Both of them are God's anointed. The king has anointing with authority the prophet has anointing with the power of the Holy Spirit. Saul lost the anointing of the Holy Spirit as a prophet because of his sin, but maintained the anointing of the Holy Spirit for authority as king. David understood this truth. When he cut Saul's garment, the Holy Spirit smote David's heart with conviction and David repented.

Spiritual Warfare Insight: Our walk will impact our ability to stand against the evil one. Do not walk in a manner that grieves the Holy Spirit. For without the Holy Spirit controlling our lives, we are powerless to stand against the enemy.

CHAPTER 4
UNDERSTANDING OUR PROTECTION IN CHRIST

We have covered the first two sections of Ephesians. The first being our position. We are in Christ. Secondly, our practice. We are to walk in a manner worthy of our calling. Now we come to the third section in Ephesians, our protection in Christ. Ephesians 6 discusses our protection in warfare. We are to put on the armor of God in order to stand against the attacks of the devil. This is definitely true in the last days when evil will abound. The Apostle Paul begins to instruct us on how to stand in the evil day.

1. STAND STRONG IN THE LORD

Ephesians 6:10 *Finally, my brethren, be strong in the Lord, and in the power of his might.* (KJV)

Notice in each section we are always connected to Christ; we are seated in Christ, we walk imitating Christ, and now we are to stand strong in the strength of Christ. This is the mystery hid from the ages "Christ in you the hope of glory".

Colossians 1:27b *...this mystery ... which is Christ in you, the hope of glory.*

We cannot stand against the powers of darkness in our own strength. We are weak, but He is strong. A great example of this is the story of Samson. He was a man who walked with God and was anointed by God. With the Lord's strength, he defended Israel and defeated the armies of the Philistines. The bible says in one day he slew a thousand Philistines with the jawbone of a donkey. That, my friend, is not natural strength, but is supernatural God given power. Yet, in his story, he sinned against God and broke the covenant. This grieved the Holy Spirit and Samson lost that anointing of power. At that point, the Philistines overtook Samson and bound him. He was defeated. What's the difference? One, he is walking in the fullness and power of the Holy Spirit and the other, he is walking in the flesh and has lost the anointed power of God.

How can I stand in the last days? By doing what Samson did. Walk in covenant with God. Put aside the sins of the flesh and walk in the fulness of the Spirit of God. That is how you stand. He is our strength, our shield and our buckler.

2. STAND STRONG IN THE FULL ARMOR OF GOD

Ephesians 6:11 *Put on the full armor of God, so that you will be able to stand firm against the schemes of the devil.*

Samson is the perfect example. He allowed the devil to use Delilah to lie and deceive him through temptation. He got caught in the devil's trap and sinned against God and lost his anointing and power. It was through lies and deception the enemy brought him down.

Understand that the devil's power is in his lies and deceptions. His deceptive schemes are to lead you to destruction. In order to stand firm against the devil's schemes we must put on the full armor of God. But before we describe the armor, it is necessary to cover a third point.

3. STAND AGAINST THE REAL ENEMY

Ephesians 6:12 *For our struggle is not against flesh and blood, but against the rulers, against the powers, against the world forces of this darkness, against the spiritual forces of wickedness in the heavenly places.*

We must stand in His strength because we are fighting a spiritual battle. We are fighting against unseen enemies. They lay snares and traps for us to step in. This is why the Apostle Paul used the word schemes. These snares and traps are planned out by the enemy. They seek to deceive us. The enemy lies to us by telling us our real battle is with a person or persons. However, that is not the case. God says it is a spiritual battle. Our fight is not against flesh and blood but against the unseen forces of evil. To be clear, these forces are demonic forces. And it doesn't matter what you have been taught. It is not just circumstances. It is not people. The bible says it is demonic forces coming against you. We must understand this principle. Otherwise, our entire life is spent fighting the wrong enemy. Therefore, prepare yourselves for battle and put on the full armor of God.

In Ephesians 6:13 Paul transitions to describing the full armor of God by using the word "therefore." Having understood our position in Christ, and our practice in Christ, let us now transition to our protection in Christ.

Ephesians 6:13 *Therefore, take up the full armor of God, so that you will be able to resist in the evil day, and having done everything, to stand firm.*

Notice, we are to put on the spiritual armor in order to resist in the evil day. That day is when the devil mounts his attack against us. The enemy's assault can take on many forms. It can come from many different directions. Paul says to put on your armor and prepare for battle. Observe the armor.

4. PUTTING ON THE ARMOR

a) Truth

Ephesians 6:14a *Stand firm therefore, HAVING GIRDED YOUR LOINS WITH TRUTH...*

It's very important that we notice where the armor starts. It starts with truth. Remember, the devil's most effective weapon is lies and deception. It just makes sense that we need to gird our loins with truth. In the old days, they would take a rope or belt and tie up their robe in order not to trip or fall. The schemes (lies) are designed to make the believer stumble and fall.

The devil is the accuser of the brethren. He tells us that God doesn't care. That God won't come through. That we are too weak and that we will never make it because the problem is too big. How do you stand against such lies? You put on truth.

Jesus is the greatest illustration. He was tempted in the wilderness for 40 days and nights. Sometimes when the devil tempted Christ, he started with the phrase "If you are the son of God..." Satan was trying to get Jesus to doubt who He was. But Jesus stood in the truth because He is truth. All the traps and temptations that the enemy brought against Jesus were not effective. Every temptation failed because Jesus chose to stand on the truth and say "It is written..."!

Remember who you are in Christ and put on truth. What is truth? God's word is truth and it is filled with great and precious promises. In life there is only one truth and that is God. Embrace what God says about you and your situation in His word and stand firm.

John 14:6 Jesus said to him, "I am the way, and the truth, and the life; no one comes to the Father but through Me.

(b) Put on the breastplate of righteousness

Ephesians 6:14 ... *and HAVING PUT ON THE BREAST-PLATE OF RIGHTEOUSNESS...*

Notice after we put on truth, we put on righteousness. Why? One of the areas that the enemy attacks most is our relationship with God. Remember, he is the accuser of the brethren. He will bring up past sins and failures and try to convince you that God has not really forgiven you. He will try to use guilt and shame to make you doubt you are right with God. This will impact you in warfare. It is hard to fight against the Devil and the forces of darkness if you are not confident that God is on your side. **That is why Paul spent so much time in the early chapters of Ephesians laying a foundation, deep and wide, on who we are in Christ.**

We must be wrapped in truth and clothed in righteousness. The word is our truth and Christ is our righteousness. We can begin preparing for the evil day by getting the word in us and knowing that Christ is our righteousness.

2 Corinthians 5:21 *He made Him who knew no sin to be sin on our behalf, so that we might become the righteousness of God in Him.*

(c) *Shod your feet*

Ephesians 6:15 ... *and having shod YOUR FEET WITH THE PREPARATION OF THE GOSPEL OF PEACE;*

The word shod means to "fit your feet". Paul is saying put the shoes on your feet that will prepare you to share the gospel of peace with others.

Romans 10:15b ... *How beautiful are the feet of them that preach the gospel of peace... (KJV)*

This is a part of the full armor of God. Having your feet ready to share Christ with people who are in need. This is a part of warfare, battling for the souls of men and women. The gospel of Christ not only affects the lost but it is good news to the saints in bondage. Remember, Moses had to contend with Pharaoh, in order for the people of Israel to be freed. God wants to use us to help free others from bondage. People all around us are being tormented by the enemy and kept in bondage and are defeated. They are unaware that the gospel of Christ gives us not only forgiveness but freedom from the kingdom of darkness and torment.

Romans 10:13 ...*for "WHOEVER WILL CALL ON THE NAME OF THE LORD WILL BE SAVED." How then will they call on Him in whom they have not believed? How will they believe in Him whom they have not heard? And how will they hear without a preacher?*

Notice the pattern that Paul gives us. It starts with putting on truth. Then he talks about putting on righteousness. You must first embrace what God has done in you; the fact that He has forgiven you, and freed you from the kingdom of darkness. Now he moves to others, to prepare your feet to share the good news with others that they too can be freed from the bondage of sin and darkness.

5. TAKE UP THE SHIELD OF FAITH

The Apostle Paul is telling us to get ready for an assault from the enemy. When you start sharing Christ, the word of God, and helping people get free, then be aware, the attacks are coming. A great example of this is Moses and Pharaoh.

God did a mighty work in the life of Moses. Then commissioned him to go to Egypt and set the people free. His confrontation was with Pharaoh. Someone getting saved or delivered from strongholds is a spiritual battle. You are contending with the devil and his forces. Remember when Moses confronted Pharaoh and Pharaoh agreed to let the people go? Pharaoh agreed that if God would lift the plague, he would set the people free. Then after the plague was removed, Pharaoh changed his mind and afflicted the people even worse. This pattern repeated itself several times. We see from this example, Moses battling the forces of darkness for the souls of men.

Ephesians 6:16 *...in addition to all, taking up the shield of faith with which you will be able to extinguish all the flaming arrows of the evil one.*

When the devil increased the torment and suffering on the people, the people turned on Moses. Moses had to take up the shield of faith to stand against the accusations of the devil and the people when they said he was the reason for their suffering. But Moses remained unmoved. He knew who he was in God. He knew he was right with God. And he knew God was with Him. Because of his knowledge of these truths, he was able to quench the fiery darts of the enemy with the shield of faith.

Our enemies shoot arrows at us. These arrows are designed to discourage and harm you. They can wound you and disable you, if they strike and hit you. Our defense is the shield of faith. What exactly does this mean? The shield of faith is trusting in God's word. Our faith is always in what God has declared.

The devil flings an arrow of accusation. You're so sinful and unworthy for God to use. We take the shield of faith and we trust what God has said about us. Through Christ all my sins have been forgiven and now I stand in His righteousness. I'm made worthy to be called a son of the Most-High God.

John 1:12 *But as many as received him, to them gave he power to become the sons of God, even to them that believe on his name* (KJV)

The shield of faith is not believing what the world says about you, nor what the devil says about you, or even what your flesh says about you. It is believing what God says about you and standing in that truth. The shield of faith will extinguish the flaming arrows of lies and wrong thinking. Faith is something we must take up and use.

6. THE HELMET OF SALVATION

Ephesians 6:17 *And take the helmet of salvation ...*

Here there are two spiritual purposes for the helmet of salvation.

a) Knowing that we are in covenant with God.

An Old Testament example was when David declared before Israel and Goliath, that Goliath was not in covenant with God. Remember David's statement when facing Goliath, the enemy's champion.

1 Samuel 17: 26b *"...For who is this uncircumcised Philistine, that he should taunt the armies of the living God?"*

David is declaring that Goliath had no relationship with the living God. Circumcision was a sign of being in covenant with the God of Abraham. David was able to stand firm, without fear, in the knowledge that God was his covenant partner. In our covenant with God, our enemies become His enemies and His enemies become ours. An attack on one, is an attack on both. This knowledge is vital in spiritual warfare. God is our covenant partner and the battle is His.

2 Chronicles 20:17b *"... Do not fear or be dismayed; tomorrow go out to face them, for the Lord is with you."*

2 Chronicles 20:15b *"Do not fear or be dismayed because of this great multitude, for the battle is not yours but God's."*

b) The battlefield of the mind

Second, the helmet of salvation indicates **where** the battle is being waged, **THE MIND**. The flaming arrows are thrown at your mind.

2 Corinthians 10:3-5 *For though we walk in the flesh, we do not war according to the flesh, for the weapons of our warfare are not of the flesh, but divinely powerful for the destruction of fortresses. We are destroying speculations and every lofty thing raised up against the knowledge of God, and we are **taking every thought captive to the obedience of Christ,***

Paul is telling us, in this battle, we must cast down every thought that is contrary to the wisdom of God. Otherwise, the lies and deception of the enemy will lead us astray into sin and disobedience. The helmet protects the head/mind. Every day we must cast down thoughts that are contrary to the wisdom of God, and embrace His Word. There are only two wisdoms in this world: the natural, demonic and Godly wisdom.

James 3:15 *This wisdom is not that which comes down from above, but is earthly, natural, demonic.*

James 3:17 *But the wisdom from above is first pure, then peaceable, gentle, reasonable, full of mercy and good fruits, unwavering, without hypocrisy.*

God is declaring in this passage, that there are only two wisdoms; wisdom which comes from above and that which is from below, the natural, demonic wisdom. In this verse, you also see that the enemy is throwing arrows at our mind. It seems as though there are three different wisdoms coming at us from beneath but if you look, they are all one. Everything from beneath is demonic.

<u>Example: In the garden of Eden there were only two wisdoms, God's and the Serpent's.</u>

Eve had to choose to believe one of the two wisdoms. One led to life and one led to death. This is what James is referring to concerning the two wisdoms. She chose to receive the wisdom from the serpent. She received it in her mind and began to reason. That was her problem. She thought she could be smarter than God. She began to trust herself and not depend on God's word. The thought led to a desire which led to a sin, which led to death. It all started when she received a thought from beneath and not from above. She should have stood on God's word and embraced His wisdom and thinking. The wisdom from above was "You can eat freely from any of the trees in the garden except this one." The fall of man goes all the way back to the battle of the mind.

Now we understand why Paul says the battle is in the mind and you have to cast down thoughts that are contrary to God. We guard our mind by casting down the wisdom from beneath and obeying the wisdom from above. Remember what Paul also said in Philippians.

Philippians 4:8 *Finally, brethren, whatever is true, whatever is honorable, whatever is right, whatever is pure, whatever is lovely, whatever is of good repute, if there is any excellence and if anything worthy of praise, dwell on these things.*

In the last days there is going to be untold pressure from this world to conform and to submit. But we must be like Daniel, Shadrach, Meshack and Abednego who refused to bend the knee to a godless empire.

In addition to taking the helmet of salvation we are also to take up the sword of the spirit.

7. THE SWORD OF THE SPIRIT

Ephesians 6:17 *And take ... the sword of the Spirit, which is the word of God.*

The sword is an offensive weapon. We are to use the word of God against the devil and the forces of evil.

Example: Jesus in the wilderness.

When Jesus was in the wilderness being tempted by the devil for 40 days, He used the word of God to combat the devil's lies and deceptive statements. Every time Jesus responded it was the same response, "it is written". The only thing we can stand on when the enemy flings the flaming arrows at us, is the word of God. The word of God is settled in heaven.

Psalms 119:89 *For ever, O LORD, thy word is settled in heaven. (KJV)*

Matthew 24:35 *"Heaven and earth will pass away, but My words will not pass away."*

Again, in this spiritual battle, we must use spiritual weapons. And the word of God is our greatest weapon against the devil. He hates the truth. He is a liar and the father of all lies.

John 8:44 *"You are of your father the devil, and you want to do the desires of your father. He was a murderer from the beginning, and does not stand in the truth because there is no truth in him. Whenever he speaks a lie, he speaks from his own nature, for he is a liar and the father of lies."*

In these last days we are to put on the full armor of God. This armor is not an outward armor but an inward armor. Things that we put on are things God is putting us; truth, righteousness, gospel of peace, faith, sword of the

Spirit which is the word of God. All of this is our inward armor. Again, this is Christ in us, the hope of glory! The bible says He is our shield, our buckler. We cannot stand on the word of God if we do not know the word of God. It is imperative that we study so that we can use the Sword of the Spirit against the enemy. This will enable us to stand firm in the evil day.

2 Timothy 2:15 *Be diligent to present yourself approved to God as a workman who does not need to be ashamed, accurately handling the word of truth.*

8. PRAYER

Notice the Apostle Paul ends the section in warfare with prayer. You may ask "What does prayer have to do with spiritual warfare against the devil?" Remember we do not wrestle against flesh and blood, but against principalities, and spiritual forces of the air, in the heavenly realm. Prayer is a spiritual force we use to move heaven and earth. How? By moving God Almighty, our Heavenly Father.

Ephesians 6:18 *With all prayer and petition pray at all times in the Spirit, and with this in view, be on the alert with all perseverance and petition for all the saints...*

Paul warns us to be alert,to be on guard, to be watchful, to be sober minded. Why? The devil lurks around trying to find a way steal, kill and destroy the believer.

1 Peter 5:8 *Be of sober spirit, be on the alert. Your adversary, the devil, prowls around like a roaring lion, seeking someone to devour.*

John 10:10a *"The thief comes only to steal and kill and destroy..."*

We are to put on the armor of God and pray diligently for one another. Warfare is all about being watchful to make sure you don't get ambushed. And also, making sure we have each other's back in the battle. In these last days we will need each other more than ever. That's why Paul ended with praying for one another.

Remember what Jesus is doing in heaven. He is sitting on the right hand of God, making intercession for each of us! He's praying for us.

Hebrews 7:25b ... *since He always lives to make intercession for them.*

Jesus is praying for us. Why? Because He knows the battle is difficult on earth, having lived it Himself. Through His compassion He chooses to pray for us every day. We need to have this kind of concern and compassion for each other. Paul is saying that in spiritual warfare you need your brothers and sisters to be in the trenches with you, praying for one another that we will be able to stand firm with each other in the evil day.

The most important thing to learn from this study is how to be prepared spiritually for the last days.

Spiritual Warfare Insight: Understanding who you are actually warring with is of utmost importance. Never forget your enemy is the demonic forces, not flesh and blood.

CHAPTER 5
SUMMARY

This book is written to help the believer stand firm in the last days. For in that day, life will be most difficult for everyone, especially believers. Listen to what God says in Jeremiah 12:

Jeremiah 12:5: *If thou hast run with the footmen, and they have wearied thee, then how canst thou contend with horses? and if in the land of peace, wherein thou trustedst, they wearied thee, then how wilt thou do in the swelling of Jordan? (KJV)*

1) If you run with the footmen and they wearied you. How can you contend with horses?

2) If in the land of peace, you are wearied. How will you do in the swelling of Jordan? (When things get really tough.)

We have to learn to stand against the forces of darkness now, so we can stand firm in the last days.

Understand your position in Christ. We are chosen. We are adopted as children. We are redeemed. We have an inheritance, the riches of Christ. This is our position and we stand in resurrection power.

1 John 4:4b ... *greater is He who is in you than he who is in the world.*

Understand your walk in practical righteousness. Make sure you stay submitted to God's authorities over you and do not walk in rebellion. Rebellion is as the sin of witchcraft and it opens the door for the enemy to attack. YOU CANNOT STAND AGAINST THE ENEMY IF YOU ARE ALIGNED WITH HIM IN REBELLION. Put off the old man and put on the new man in Christ.

Understand your warfare and put on Christ. This requires putting on the full armor of God. Then taking a stand against the devil and his forces. Also, using your offensive weapons to help free others from the bondage of sin and the devil. Remember, prayer is a mighty weapon against the kingdom of darkness. Intercede for one another. Pray for each other diligently with perseverance, being on alert and watchful for the enemy's tactics to defeat us.

How does one prepare for the last days? You prepare spiritually. Keep your eyes on the Lord and stand firm against evil.

It is my prayer that God will take this teaching in Ephesians and will strengthen and encourage you in your walk with Christ.

ABOUT THE AUTHOR

Terry Bryant has been a minister of the Gospel of Jesus Christ for 49 years. He was saved at the age of 18. He married Sherry in 1975 and they are the proud parents of 11 children. He has served as youth minister, and pastored several churches. He also served 6 years as a missionary in Haiti. Terry was in country when the Haitian government was overthrown and the whole country erupted in killings and chaos. He has been a street evangelist, and carried a 10 foot cross through the state of Alabama. He preached Resurrection rallies on all the major and minor college campuses, and has been a national conference speaker. Dr Fred Wolfe was his mentor throughout his ministry. There have been several Godly individuals that have impacted his life, including Jack Taylor, Peter Lord, Leonard Ravenhill, James Robinson, and Ms. Bertha Smith. His desire now is to write books and share God's insights with the next generation.

You have a story.
We want to publish it.

Everyone has as a story to tell. It might be about something you know how to do, or what has happened in your life, or it may be a thrilling, or romantic, or intriguing, or heartwarming, or suspenseful story, starring a cast of characters that have been swimming around in your imagination.

And at Wyatt House Publishing, we can get your story onto the pages of a book just like the one you are holding in your hand. With professional interior design and a custom, professionally designed cover built just for you from the start, you can finally see your dream of being an author become reality. Then, you will see your book listed with retailers all over the world as people are able to buy your book from wherever they are and have it delivered to their home or their e-reader.

So what are you waiting for? This is your time.

visit us at

www.wyattpublishing.com

for details on how to get started becoming a
published author right away.

www.ingramcontent.com/pod-product-compliance
Lightning Source LLC
Chambersburg PA
CBHW031401060726
47590CB00007B/2899